It Is
and
Big Fin and Fat Ben

Level 1 – Pink

Helpful Hints for Reading at Home

The graphemes (written letters) and phonemes (units of sound) used throughout this series are aligned with Letters and Sounds. This offers a consistent approach to learning whether reading at home or in the classroom.

HERE IS A LIST OF NEW PHONEMES FOR THIS PHASE OF LEARNING. AN EXAMPLE OF THE PRONUNCIATION CAN BE FOUND IN BRACKETS.

Phase 2			
s (sat)	a (cat)	t (tap)	p (tap)
i (pin)	n (net)	m (man)	d (dog)
g (go)	o (sock)	c (cat)	k (kin)
ck (sack)	e (elf)	u (up)	r (rabbit)
h (hut)	b (ball)	f (fish)	ff (off)
l (lip)	ll (ball)	ss (hiss)	

HERE ARE SOME WORDS WHICH YOUR CHILD MAY FIND TRICKY.

Phase 2 Tricky Words			
the	to	I	no
go	into		

TOP TIPS FOR HELPING YOUR CHILD TO READ:

• Allow children time to break down unfamiliar words into units of sound and then encourage children to string these sounds together to create the word.

• Encourage your child to point out any focus phonics when they are used.

• Read through the book more than once to grow confidence.

• Ask simple questions about the text to assess understanding.

• Encourage children to use illustrations as prompts.

PHASE 2 /f/

This book focuses on the phoneme /f/ and is a pink level 1 book band.

It Is A...
and
Big Fin and Fat Ben

Written by
Gemma McMullen &
Rod Barkman

Illustrated by
Farah Shah &
Danielle Webster-Jones

Can you say this sound and draw it with your finger?

It Is A...

Written by
Rod Barkman

Illustrated by
Danielle Webster-Jones

It is a man.

It is a tin.

It is a dog.

It is a pig.

It is a cog.

It is a bin.

It is a cot.

It is a dot.

It is a pot.

It is a map.

It is a cat.

It is fun.

Can you make it through the maze to collect the letter f? How many objects beginning with f can you collect along the way?

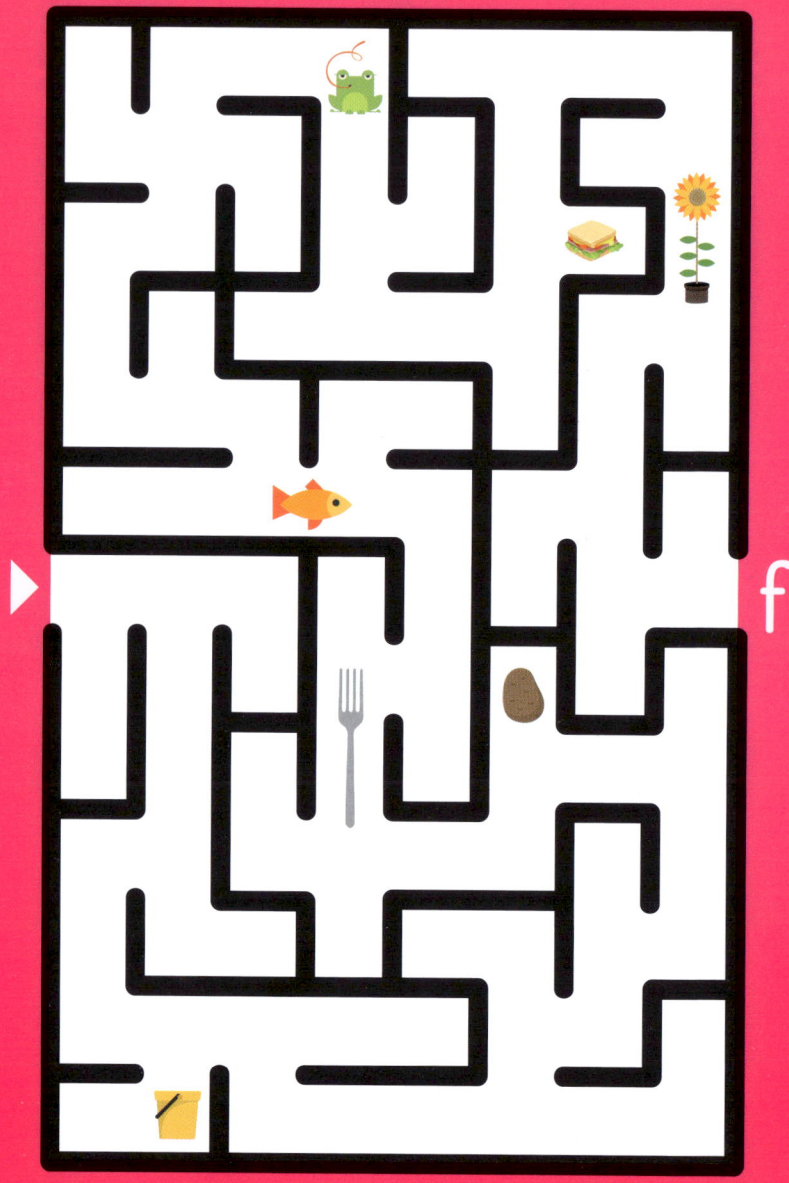

Big Fin and Fat Ben

Written by
Gemma McMullen

Illustrated by
Farah Shah

Big Fin and Fat Ben.

Big Fin is fit.

Fat Ben is not.

Fat Ben is hot.

Huff and puff, Ben.

Big Fin is not hot.

Fin hops off.

Big Fin in the fog.

Fin is sad.

Fat Ben hops in.

Big Fin and Fat Ben.

Fin and Ben had fun.

©2021 BookLife Publishing Ltd.
King's Lynn, Norfolk PE30 4LS

ISBN 978-1-83927-863-1

All rights reserved. Printed in Malta.
A catalogue record for this book is available from the British Library.

It Is A...
Written by Gemma McMullen
Illustrated by Danielle Webster-Jones
Big Fin and Fat Ben
Written by Gemma McMullen
Illustrated by Farah Shah

An Introduction to BookLife Readers...

Our Readers have been specifically created in line with the London Institute of Education's approach to book banding and are phonetically decodable and ordered to support each phase of the Letters and Sounds document.

Each book has been created to provide the best possible reading and learning experience. Our aim is to share our love of books with children, providing both emerging readers and prolific page-turners with beautiful books that are guaranteed to provoke interest and learning, regardless of ability.

BOOK BAND GRADED using the Institute of Education's approach to levelling.

PHONETICALLY DECODABLE supporting each phase of Letters and Sounds.

EXERCISES AND QUESTIONS to offer reinforcement and to ascertain comprehension.

BEAUTIFULLY ILLUSTRATED to inspire and provoke engagement, providing a variety of styles for the reader to enjoy whilst reading through the series.

AUTHOR INSIGHT: GEMMA MCMULLEN

Gemma McMullen is one of BookLife Publishing's most multi-faceted and talented individuals. Born in Newport, Gwent, she studied at the University of Northampton, where she graduated with a BA (Hons) in English and Drama. She then attended the University of Wales where she obtained her PGCE Primary qualification, and has been teaching ever since. Her experience as a teacher enables her to find exactly what makes children focus and learn, and allows her to write books that amuse and fascinate their readers.

This book focuses on the phoneme /f/ and is a pink level 1 book band.